Praise for *Blue Collar*

If you are crazy enough to think you can be your own boss, and ever have second thoughts about that decision, this book will: remind you why you believe it, silence the voices of doubters creeping back into your thoughts, and shine a light on the path that will prove you were right all along. At least it did for me.

—Pablo Gonzalez, Host, B2B Community Builder Show
and co-founder of BeTheStage.live

If you like business *and* struggle to read business books, you will *love Blue Collar Entrepreneur*! Brett shares practical, hands-on wisdom from the "rugged plains of reality" of his own story. It is a page turner - you will see yourself in Brett's story and identify areas for growth in your own journey.

—Steven Neuner, Author of Dogs on Heaven Street,
and Leadership Coach

BLUE-COLLAR ENTREPRENEUR

9 Principles for Building a Business That Works *for* You

BRETT RUIZ

WITH ERIN CASEY

ethos
collective

Published by Ethos Collective™

PO Box 43, Powell, OH 43065

EthosCollective.vip

LCCN:

Paperback ISBN: 978-1-63680-082-0

Hardback ISBN: 978-1-63680-083-7

e-book ISBN: 978-1-63680-084-4

Printed in the United States of America.

Available in paperback, e-book, and audiobook

CONTENTS

INTRODUCTION
HOW'S THAT WORKING FOR YOU?

*No person will make a great business who wants
to do it all himself or get all the credit.*

—Andrew Carnegie

"Dude, it looks like you have the weight of the world on your shoulders."

Is it that obvious? I wondered. I had just arrived at my networking group's annual meeting when Mark greeted me with his observation.

Shaking Mark's hand, I replied, "Yeah, I sure do." I didn't want to get into it right then—or really ever—so I quickly moved on to find a seat before the first session started.

As the owner of a young company, I had gotten used to handling everything myself. I was CEO, CFO, CMO, and COO. If there had been another C-hat to add at the time, I would have been wearing that one too. This setup had worked for a while—sort of—but with our growth, the hours and responsibilities had gotten way out of hand. I still made time for my family, but balancing family time with work and making time for my church and spiritual life had me stretched in all directions. I could manage to do each in spurts but hadn't found a rhythm that allowed me to balance it all at the same time.

My company, Medina Exteriors, had grown from its early start—with a cordless phone and old elementary school desk under a pull-chain light in the basement—to one that people in the area knew and trusted. Repeat customers, referrals, and a massive amount of hustle had resulted in more work than we could handle—or afford. The company was $100,000 in debt, and I was robbing Peter to pay Paul. My ego and pride had taken over, and I kept thinking I could sell my way out of the problem.

Truthfully, it wasn't any wonder the finances were a mess. I barely had time to pay attention to the books. Between making sales calls to drum up new business and managing the company's heavy project load, there just weren't enough hours in the day. And what was I thinking trying to handle the finances in the first place? I couldn't even balance a checkbook in high school. The company had been up and running full-steam for about eight years, and I constantly felt like I was racing to keep up with everything.

My sense of responsibility (and let's be honest, my pride) wouldn't let me ask for help. After all, I was the boss. The buck stopped with me, so it was my responsibility to make things right.

I had put everything on the line to make my business a reality. My wife had quit her job to stay home with our four young children (my idea), so not only was the company's success in jeopardy, but my livelihood and my family's financial security were also at risk.

And I was failing.

Joining the networking group squeezed my already overloaded schedule, but I went with the hope of finding some fresh ideas or inspiration. Mostly, I needed a solution—or a bigger shovel to dig myself out of the hole I'd gotten myself into (even though I did not realize when I joined the group just how deep that hole was).

Instead of feeling better, being there made me feel worse. Mark's stinging, truthful words sparked my already short fuse. Listening to others at the meeting talk about their thriving businesses only increased the stress, fear, and anger I felt. On the upside, hearing them talk about their failures let me know that I could be vulnerable without fearing their judgement.

My emotional pressure valve finally broke while I was in a goal-setting session. The president of the networking group and leader for the workshop, Monroe Porter, knew me and my business pretty well, and like everyone else in the room, he noticed the stress that was weighing me down. During that session, he gave me the name of another business owner at the meeting who might have some suggestions for me.

My ego wasn't having it. I didn't want someone else's suggestions. When I told him I would figure things out on my own, he called me out.

"Did you hear that, Bud?" Monroe asked a guy sitting nearby. "Brett thinks he knows everything and says he doesn't need any help."

"Yep, that sounds about right," Bud said.

"How's that working for you, Brett?" Monroe asked.

The other men in the room chuckled.

That stress, fear, and anger that had been building during the conference (and honestly, for the past couple of years) threatened to explode. Tears began to sting my eyes. Not wanting to bawl in front of seven other guys, all of whom were in the construction industry, I decided to get out of there—fast. I stood up and walked to the first door I came to.

I opened it and, without stopping, walked right into a coat closet.

You've got to be kidding me.

I shut the door behind me, unwilling to go back out there and let all those guys watch me lose it.

A few minutes later, I heard a knock on the door. It was Monroe and Bud. I opened the door expecting to face further humiliation, but thankfully, everybody else had left the room. Now slightly calmer, I stepped out of the closet. Monroe, Bud, and I found a place to talk, and over the next few hours, we worked out a game plan to get my business and my life back on track.

Overwhelm vs. Abundance

So many entrepreneurs, maybe including you, feel just as over-whelmed, stressed out, and fearful as I did that day in the closet. They're doing all they can to keep up with the demands and responsibilities of leading a company. They work non-stop, all day, every day, and most nights, but they can't seem to get the business under control. Instead, the business controls them.

Others desperately want to own and run successful businesses, but no matter what they do or how many ideas they've pursued, nothing seems to work out the way they had hoped. Time after time their startups fail and never become viable, sustainable ventures.

I understand their frustration because I've been there. Medina Exteriors wasn't my first business. It took me a number of failures to find the right fit, and once I found it, I almost ran myself into the ground trying to build it.

Today, I mentor and coach new entrepreneurs who are in the same place I was all those years ago. They're stressed out and over-whelmed, in large part because they're trying to do everything themselves. If that's you, then I'll ask you the same question that sent me to the coat closet: How's that working for you?

If you're tempted to respond with something like, "I've got everything under control," then take a look at the list below and check the box beside anything that sounds familiar:

- ☐ You are working more hours than you want to, but you always feel behind.
- ☐ You are bringing in sales, but your profit margin is slim to non-existent.
- ☐ You wish you could clone yourself so you could be in the office and in the field at the same time.
- ☐ No one on your team can do the job (any job) quite as well as you, so you keep wearing all the hats.
- ☐ You can't remember the last time you took two days in a row completely off (no phone, no email, no work at all).

☐ You are handling tasks on a regular basis that drain you and take you out of your area of excellence.

☐ You are one crisis away from losing it all. If you got sick or hurt, or had to shut down for a week or a month, your business couldn't recover.

☐ You know your current pace isn't sustainable. You are aware that you need to make some changes, but you have no idea where to start or what to do differently.

☐ You are working *for your business* when you know it should be working *for you*.

Few people become entrepreneurs because they think it's the easy route. If you've already started a business, then chances are good that you knew it would be hard work—just not this hard. If you checked off any (or all) of the statements in that list, then *The Blue-Collar Entrepreneur* is your invitation to turn things around and move from overwhelmed to abundance. Most, if not all, of the issues listed above come back to one of three common needs for any entrepreneur:

- People
- Processes
- Technology

Like a three-legged stool, these elements work together to support you as an entrepreneur so you can have the freedom and abundance of time you desire.

The good news is that if you get the right processes in place, then it's easier to find the right people. If you have the right people in place and use technology that allows you and your team to automate tasks, then time freedom becomes possible. Bottom line: No matter how overwhelmed and overworked you feel right now, you can have a business that you love—a business that works for you.

I built my career in the construction industry. In the past thirty years, the company has expanded from Medina Exteriors to Medina Exteriors & Remodeling + Simply Distinct Kitchen and

Baths. We've earned a reputation in Northeast Ohio for exceptional quality work and stellar customer service, and I'm proud of what our team and I have learned and accomplished. The stories I'll share with you come from my experiences in this industry, but the universal principles they reveal apply to almost any entrepreneurial endeavor.

No matter what industry you're in, you'll find practical advice here that will help you avoid entrepreneurial disasters and recover from failures faster. (Because it's not *if* you make mistakes, it's *when*. You're going to make mistakes—that's guaranteed.)

You'll also get in-the-trenches insight that will equip you to build a strong foundation for a business so you can create the freedom you hoped for when you first had the idea to become an entrepreneur. The change won't happen overnight or without work. Getting to a place that provides you with both financial freedom and freedom of time is a journey. Along the way, you will face struggles and challenges. My hope is that you'll allow me to join you on that journey and that, together, we can make your path a little smoother.

I know the path to entrepreneurship can feel like one made of wet concrete. You wade out into it alone only to discover it's the quick-set kind, and it's drying all around you. You feel scared, stuck, or maybe even suffocated. But you don't have to stay that way.

This book is a tool to help you break free from that concrete so you can carve a path to freedom and abundance. And even though you're the one driving the business, you don't have to go it alone. Yes, you're the one with the vision, and everyone in your company is looking to you for direction. And yes, it can feel lonely at the top. But you aren't alone. I'm here offering you a lifetime of experience, a community of support, and nine applicable principles to help you thrive as an entrepreneur.

Now, doesn't that sound a whole lot better than being stuck in concrete?

If you were on my team, then I'd tell you to grab your tools and get over to the jobsite.

Let's get to work.

Application

Look back at that list on page XX. What are the top three issues you're facing right now?

1. _____

2. _____

3. _____

CHAPTER 1
HOW DO YOU KNOW YOU'RE AN ENTREPRENEUR?

*Don't let other's opinions drown out your own inner voice.
Have the courage to follow your heart and intuition.*

—Steve Jobs

*No one is ever going to control my life or my destiny or tell me where
I have to be ever again.* The thoughts came in a flood as I hurried
through the halls of Akron General Hospital to my son's room.
With each fluorescent light that passed overhead, I thought, *Never
again. This is it. I'm done working for someone else.*

It was 1992, long before the age of mobile phones and
hyper-connectedness. It had been a long day at work, and I was
thankful to be home. I pulled into my driveway and was just about
to go into the house when my sister-in-law met me at the front door.

"Don't panic," she said.

It's never good when someone starts a conversation that way.

"Why? What happened? What's wrong?"

"Chris and Deanna are at the hospital," she began.

My mind flooded with worst-nightmare type thoughts as she gave me the quick version of the story. Chris, our six-year-old son, had drowned and had to be revived and then taken by Lifeflight to Akron General. He was okay but under observation as a precaution.

Before racing to the hospital, I called my boss to let him know I wouldn't be at work the next day. I explained there had been an accident and my son was in the hospital. Unbelievably, the guy gave me a hard time about missing my shift. I hung up the phone, sick with worry for my little boy and angry at my boss for being less than empathetic. Scratch that—he was a jerk about it.

I shortened the thirty-five-minute drive across town to just fifteen. I parked and hurried to the room where my wife sat with our little boy. I was expecting to find him unconscious with tubes coming in and out of his little body. To my surprise, he was awake when I entered the room and said, "Hey, Dad," and smiled.

While I hugged them both, my wife, Deanna, told me the whole story. Chris had been out riding his bike and playing with some friends when they all stopped at a culvert in our neighborhood. We'd had a lot of rain that season, and the deep ditch ran full with drain off. One of the things the kids loved to do was throw sticks into the water from one side of the bridge and then cross the street and watch for them to come out the other side. Chris had done that a hundred times before, but this time, he leaned too far over the edge and lost his balance.

He fell into the water below, and at only six, he didn't yet know how to swim.

The other kids started yelling for help, and by God's provision, a neighbor who had come home early that day heard their panicked screams. She could tell the cries were more than just kids out playing—something was wrong. She ran over and asked what had happened.

Still screaming, the kids pointed to where our son had fallen into the culvert. Catching a glimpse of his new, bright-white tennis shoes just beneath the surface of the murky water, the woman dove in and pulled him out. By the time they emerged, another neighbor had called 911 and a police cruiser had pulled up. The officer took our son, who was limp and not breathing, and performed CPR to resuscitate him.

By the time Chris had revived, the neighborhood was screaming with sirens. Deanna, who had been at home in the backyard, heard the commotion and ran to see what was wrong. Imagine her shock when she saw our little boy wrapped in a blanket and being tended to by the medical team. A few minutes later, a helicopter landed and took them both to the hospital.

Listening to the machines beep and whir as Deanna relayed the story, I couldn't stop thanking God that our little boy was alive.

That day was a turning point for me. When my boss hassled me for taking a day off to be with my son after the accident, a spark ignited deep within me. I had always suspected I wasn't designed for a typical career path. I wanted to be in control of my life, my time, and my destiny. The brief phone call with my boss and the emotion of the day had affirmed to me something I had felt for a long time but hadn't yet put into words: I was an entrepreneur at heart. I wanted to work for myself.

This realization didn't shock me. Even as a child, I looked at the world differently than my peers did. I constantly tinkered with things—from toys to my bike and later, my moped—to try to make them better. When I was a young teen mowing lawns for money, I developed systems to make edging and mowing more efficient. Rather than joining the local little league with all its rules and fees, the neighborhood kids and I made our own baseball club.

If there was a better, faster, or more interesting way to do something, I was going to find it.

My upbringing played right into that natural bent to innovate and improvise. I had a great, upper-middle-class childhood, but my parents didn't hover over or coddle me. I learned early on that if I wanted something done, then I needed to take responsibility and do it myself.

Having to figure things out on my own also taught me persistence. If something didn't work out on the first attempt, I tried again. And again. When I was fifteen, I applied that persistence to getting a job at a local restaurant. I turned in an application, and after a day or two had passed, I called to check in and see about getting an interview. The manager told me she hadn't had a chance to look at my application yet and to call again the next day. I did, and I got the same response. So I called again the next day, and the next.

Seven days and seven phone calls later, the manager said, "Your persistence has paid off. I'm going to hire you."

I started the next day at the very bottom rung—cleaning bathrooms. It wasn't glamorous, but it was a start.

Those traits of innovation, independence, self-reliance, persistence, and the desire to make the world better served me well throughout my early years and adulthood. And they are essential traits for an entrepreneur.

Not Everyone Is Going to *Get* You (and That's Okay)

Not everyone *gets* entrepreneurs. You may have experienced this reality firsthand if you've ever offered up an idea and gotten a deer-in-the-headlights stare in return. When I was a kid, my friends didn't understand why I couldn't just let things be—I always wanted to make stuff better. As a student, I hated wasting time on subjects that seemed irrelevant. Later, as an employee, my bosses didn't appreciate that I regularly questioned why things were done a particular way when another way would be faster, cheaper, or more effective.

Much of the world is just fine with the status quo, happy to plug along doing the same thing day after day while working for someone else. But not me, and not you—at least, not if you're an entrepreneur.

One gift success has provided me with is the opportunity to speak to, coach, and mentor people who aren't as far along their career path as I am. I enjoy these opportunities because I wish someone had done the same thing for me.

Occasionally, young people or those who are considering transitioning out of the corporate world into their own business ventures will reach out to me for advice. Whether they're just starting out or are launching into their second act, one question tends to surface consistently in our conversations:

Do I have what it takes to be an entrepreneur?

It's a fair question because, honestly, not everyone is cut out to be an entrepreneur, and that's okay. The world needs all kinds of workers. Unfortunately, many people want the perceived freedom and ease of working for themselves but fail to factor in what their business is going to require of them.

You're here, reading this book, because you either are or want to be an entrepreneur. Maybe you're still in the dreaming and planning stage, or maybe you've already started your business and are just far enough in to wonder, *What have I gotten myself into? Do I have what it takes to make this business a success?*

Let's take a look at the most common traits of successful entrepreneurs and find out.

Principle 1: Understand the Entrepreneurial Mindset

The traits that follow are some of those that make entrepreneurs successful. Going out on your own in business isn't always easy—in fact, it rarely is. You need the fortitude and the grit to get through hard times and the instincts to know when to reach even higher. In other words, if you want to succeed as an entrepreneur, then you need the mindset of an entrepreneur. Here's what that mindset looks like:

- **Entrepreneurs are self-motivated.** They don't need someone to tell them to get to work—they're already there! That motivation is often driven by a personal mission or passion. They are excited to start each new day because they know they are making a difference with their work for the betterment of the world around them.

- **Entrepreneurs have big ideas.** They can see beyond their present circumstances and envision what could be. Some people see them as dreamers or fanciful, and to some extent, that may be true. It takes a big vision to make a big difference.
- **Entrepreneurs are persistent.** Rejection is part of the game for business builders. They aren't afraid of hearing no, because they realize every no leads them closer to a yes. They refuse to quit when things get hard, because they believe the payoff is worth the effort and the world needs what they are offering.
- **Entrepreneurs take risks often.** Entrepreneurship isn't for the risk-averse. Those who launch out on their own know they are taking a risk from Day One. They know that growth frequently requires stepping out in faith, but it isn't blind faith. Smart entrepreneurs do their homework and are agile and flexible enough to pivot when needed to keep the business moving forward.
- **Entrepreneurs are committed to continual learning and improvement.** There's no such thing as a stagnant entrepreneur. Good enough is never good enough. Entrepreneurs become experts in their field because they are always learning and trying new things. They are committed to doing things better today than they did yesterday.
- **Entrepreneurs aren't afraid of going it alone but would rather bring others along for the ride.** Many businesses start from very humble beginnings, with one person who has an idea and the work ethic to make their dream a reality. Growth, however, usually requires collaboration with and support from others who can expand the company's knowledge and skill base. Entrepreneurs wisely invite others into the business when they are ready to scale up.
- **Entrepreneurs are innovative and creative.** They are able to look at the world, their job, or the task at hand from

multiple angles. They can see ways to do things better or more efficiently. They welcome obstacles as opportunities to find solutions for the business and its customers. They see "that's the way we've always done it" as a challenge to do things differently.

- **Entrepreneurs have a positive, abundance mindset.** They believe and expect that things can always be better. They anticipate success and prepare for it. They practice possibility thinking by staying focused on the future while making the most of the present. They operate from an abundance mindset, believing that there is plenty of success for everyone to share.
- **Entrepreneurs take responsibility.** Ownership of the business means ownership of everything related to the business—the successes and the failures. Entrepreneurs are intent on creating positive experiences for their customers and employees, and when something doesn't go right, they do what it takes to fix it.
- **Entrepreneurs are resilient.** Entrepreneurship and failure go hand in hand. Dreaming big, taking risks, and pushing for the untried and innovative naturally carries the potential for failure. Sometimes recovery is simple. Other times mistakes, miscalculations, and unforeseen circumstances can bring the business to a sudden stop. Entrepreneurs know how to tap into their resiliency, collaborate with others, get up, pivot, and start again.

Application

Do you have what it takes to be an entrepreneur? Take a look at the list of entrepreneurial traits below and put a check mark by each characteristic you feel you possess.

- ☐ Self-motivated
- ☐ Visionary
- ☐ Persistent

- ☐ Willing to take risks
- ☐ Continual learner
- ☐ Committed to improvement
- ☐ Self-starter
- ☐ Able to work with or lead others
- ☐ Innovative/Creative
- ☐ Positive and abundant mindset
- ☐ Possibility focused
- ☐ Willing to take responsibility for both actions and outcomes
- ☐ Resilient

What other traits do you have that might make you a good entrepreneur?

_____

_____

CHAPTER 2
FALSE STARTS

An entrepreneurial culture thrives when it's easy to try lots of new ideas. The greatest successes come from having the freedom to fail.

—**Mark Zuckerberg**

I wish someone had come alongside me in high school or as I was going into college and talked to me about what it meant to an entrepreneur. Today, universities offer courses and degrees in entrepreneurship and small-business ownership, but back then, those options didn't exist. (Even though the options are better for today's students, the reality is that most of the professors teaching about entrepreneurship have never lived the life. They're teaching from theory rather than practice, which is why I believe mentors and networking are essential. More on that in chapter 5.)

When it came time for me to decide what to do after high school, I didn't feel like I had any option other than to go to college. All my friends were choosing their schools, and every adult I knew had followed the typical path from high school graduation to college to an entry-level job. They had started at the bottom and worked their way up. My parents didn't force me to go to college, but they, and all my friends, assumed I would. It went against every fiber of my being, but I succumbed to the pressure I felt to conform and started down that well-worn, traditional route to responsible adulthood.

It didn't take long for me to realize that college wasn't for me. Just as I had in grade school, middle school, and high school, I hated wasting time on coursework that seemed to have no purpose or use. Added to that was the pressure of trying to decide what I wanted to do with my life—*for the rest of my life*. Who knows that at eighteen? I certainly didn't.

One of the things that bugged me about school was that I couldn't see the reward in it. As I said, every adult I knew had taken the traditional college-to-career path, but no one really seemed excited about their work. Beyond that, I noticed a pervasive scarcity mindset that just didn't match up with the way I thought about life.

I went to college because I was supposed to, and after two years, I called it quits. I still didn't know what I wanted to do with my life, but I knew I had to do something different.

(The one good thing that came out of my short-lived college experience was reconnecting with Deanna. We had gone to grade school together, but back then, she didn't give me a second glance. Thankfully, in college, things were a different story. We ended up getting married in 1989.)

After leaving college, I went into the National Guard, but that also turned out to be a very bad fit. I served a few years of what was supposed to be a longer term, but ultimately, I was released with a general discharge because it was clear to me and the staff sergeant that my independent mindset wasn't a good match for the military. Authority and I just couldn't seem to get along. It wasn't that I had a problem with authority—I just wanted to have control over my life, and I didn't like people telling me what to do and where to be.

Now I was back to trying to create my own path, and I still didn't know which direction to go—so I tried all of them.

Throughout high school, I had worked in a restaurant, where I moved up from toilet-cleaner to head cook before I left for college. After leaving the military, I needed a job to pay the rent, so I went back to working in a restaurant. The hospitality industry wasn't my passion, but people were, and serving customers honed my people skills. I knew I didn't want to work in a restaurant forever, though, so I always had another gig or business idea going on the side.

I bought an auto-detailing franchise.

I bought exercise equipment and opened a small gym.

I sold high-end vacuum cleaners.

I became a sales rep for TruGreen Lawn Service.

I sold life insurance for Primerica.

I bought and sold rental properties.

Every six to twelve months, I switched jobs. What I wanted was something that fit me well and allowed me to make a difference somehow in people's lives. Each new venture provided me with income, so in some respects, all of them were successful, but none felt exactly right for me. I'd start with enthusiasm and then either lose interest, find a flaw in the plan, or simply realize the business wasn't a good match for me.

What might have looked like failure to others was really preparation for my future. It's because of all those false starts and my willingness to try new things that I eventually found the industry and the business I loved.

I was tending bar at a restaurant when a regular customer offered me a part-time job with his window and siding business. I knew nothing about the industry, but that wasn't about to stop me. We shook hands over the bar, and I started working for him the next week.

Why Can't You Keep a Job?

Those early years weren't easy for my wife. I drove her crazy with all my ideas. She needed security and stability, and there I was constantly jumping from one new opportunity to the next. From the outside looking in, I'm sure people thought I couldn't make up my mind about what I wanted to do, and maybe that was partly true. I liked trying on different things to see what fit—and what didn't.

Looking back with the understanding that I've had an entrepreneurial spirit all my life, it's not surprising that college was one of those things that didn't fit. A CNBC survey shows that only 44 percent of entrepreneurs have a college degree.[1] Entrepreneurs are dreamers and possibility thinkers. It's important to learn from history, but for people like me—and that probably includes you—the future is what's most important. Academia focuses on what has worked in the past, but for entrepreneurs, who are constantly improving and growing, real-life, hands-on learning quickly surpasses the best practices printed in outdated textbooks.

As for all the new business ideas I tried, what can I say? Sometimes I dove into a new venture because I thought I could do the job better or more profitably than others. Other times I just wanted to see if I could do it. When a job or a business stopped making sense for me, I wouldn't see any reason to continue down that path, so I'd quit and look for something else.

For some entrepreneurs, it takes awhile to find the right company, product, or industry. Others refuse to pick just one. Serial entrepreneurs launch and build multiple businesses throughout their careers. Some build their companies and then sell them off to pursue something new. Others, like Sir Richard Branson, Elon Musk, and the late Steve Jobs, simultaneously operate several companies in a wide variety of industries.

The curiosity and creativity that are ingrained into the entrepreneurial mindset make trying new things both fun and necessary. So go for it. Take risks. Try something new. And remember that it's okay to fail.

Principle 2: Fail Frequently. Fail Fast. Fail Forward.

What I didn't realize at the time was that those false starts were part of the process of failing frequently, failing fast, and failing forward. Finally, when I was twenty-six, I came across something that fit and began traveling the path that led to where I am now. There were plenty of diversions along the way, but they all pointed in the same general direction. There were also plenty of failures to learn from even after I had found the industry I wanted to focus on.

Nobody likes the idea of failure. It seems so final. The truth, however, is that failure is an essential part of success. Failure is so important that Google incorporated "Never Fail to Fail" into its principles of innovation.[2] Gopi Kallayil, Google's Chief Evangelist for Brand Marketing, noted early in the company's formation that "Failure is the way to be innovative and successful. You can fail with pride." The trick is to fail fast, or, in other words, to be willing to acknowledge what isn't working, shift gears, and try something else.[3]

Rather than attempting to avoid failure, recognize that it's going to happen and make the choice to fail frequently, fail fast, and fail forward.

Fail frequently. When you're just starting out, trying a variety of new things helps you identify what you like and what you don't like. When you're building a business, allowing yourself to fail frequently gives you the freedom to experiment.

At my company, we constantly look for ways to improve the customer experience and the quality of our work, and we are always open to testing new products and processes that move us toward that goal. Sometimes those experiments work out. Other times they don't and we move on and try something else. We repeat the process and keep only the very best practices.

Fail fast. Failing fast is also about freedom—freedom to stop doing what isn't working. During the times when I was trying my hand at detailing cars or running a gym, my restaurant jobs served as my financial backup. If a new endeavor didn't work out, it was okay. I could still pay my bills by tending bar, waiting tables, or working in the kitchen, which removed some of the pressure to succeed and made it fun to try new things. It also gave me the option to quit if something wasn't working out.

The same is true for the new things we try today at Medina Exteriors & Remodeling and Simply Distinct Kitchen and Baths.

When we order from a new vendor or put someone in a new role, we allow ourselves a testing period. If, for any reason, the change isn't a good fit or doesn't provide the solution we had hoped for, it's not the end of the world. Our company is agile enough that we can quickly evaluate whether or not something is worth continuing, and if it's not, we stop. Typically, we can go back to the last thing that worked and continue doing that until a potentially better idea comes along.

Some people say that winners never quit. I prefer business expert Seth Godin's take: "Winners quit all the time. They just quit the right stuff at the right time."[4]

Fail forward. When you're running a business, failure is inevitable. In the process of continually improving and growing, you're going to try things that don't work. Team members (and even you) will make mistakes from time to time. Failure is part of life—particularly the entrepreneurial life—and that's good news. It means you will regularly have opportunities to learn and improve, or, in other words, to fail forward.

There's a saying that holds true for business and for life: "Success isn't final and failure isn't fatal. It's the courage to continue that counts." It doesn't matter how many times you fail, as long as you learn from each experience and keep pressing forward.

The US Bureau of Labor Statistics reports that 20 percent of new businesses fail within the first year. Fifty percent fail by year five.[5] Let's put those statistics in a new light: 80 percent of new businesses make it to the one-year mark. That's pretty encouraging! Even if your business is among the 20 percent, remember that failure isn't necessarily a bad thing. It means you've identified what didn't work. Failure forces you to reassess your motives, the market, and the end goal—something all business owners should do. Going through that evaluation gives you clarity about yourself and the business's needs, which sets you up for future success.

Try, fail, learn, pivot, try again. That's the pattern that will lead you to success.

Application

- Have you tried anything new lately?
- What are you doing now that you need to quit?
- What is one thing your last failure taught you?

CHAPTER 3
THE (REAL) BEGINNING

Imperfect action beats perfect inaction every time.
—**President Harry S. Truman**

"Why don't you start your own business?" Mike asked.

It was a good question, and one that I had been seriously considering.

Even before that day in the hospital with my son, I had been thinking about what it would take to launch out on my own. I had been selling for the window and siding company for a few months, and I really loved the industry. Going into someone's home and helping increase its value by making it more attractive and more energy efficient felt good because I knew I was making a difference.

I had learned the ropes and paid attention to how the business ran. I knew how to sell windows and siding and that I would need to hire and pay subcontractors to do the work. What I didn't know was how to open my own company. The only thing I had to invest was my time and commitment. Unfortunately, supplies, office space, and trucks—things I assumed I needed before I could get started—cost money, something I didn't have much of at the time.

Mike was a friend from church who worked in a similar industry. He had told me almost a year earlier to reach out if I ever needed a job. I took him up on the offer thinking he would have me start selling for his company. It wouldn't have been the same as working for myself, but it might be a step or two closer.

Rather than giving me a job with his company, however, Mike encouraged me to start my own and even offered to help me get it off the ground.

I didn't have to think too long. I was in! "Let's do it," I told him. "What do I do first?"

"Make some appointments," he replied.

So I did.

We lived in Medina, Ohio, and I was going to sell siding and roofing, so I decided to name my brand-new business Medina Exteriors. (I wasn't even sure I could use this name for the company, but I ran with it anyway.)

I got my Criss Cross Directory (which served as an analog database) and set up a school desk, a creaky chair, and a floor lamp with a pull chain in the basement. It turned out those things and our cordless phone were all I needed to start the business. I sat down and started dialing.

Mike had given me some scripts to follow as I cold-called potential customers from the directory. Within a few hours, I had made three appointments for the next day: one at 12:00 p.m., one at 3:00 p.m., and one at 6:00 p.m.

Now what? I wondered.

I called Mike again. "Listen, man, I just set up three appointments."

He chuckled into the phone, picking up on the mix of excitement and trepidation in my voice. "Don't worry," he said. "I'll go with you tomorrow. I'll pick you up and bring some samples with me."

What I hadn't realized was that Mike was a distributor for a windows, siding, and roofing vendor.

By the time we hung up, it was getting late in the evening. I wanted my new company to look established and legitimate to the prospects we would be meeting with the next day, which meant I needed a contract in the event someone decided to buy from me. Of course, since my business wasn't even twenty-four hours old, I didn't have a contract. I also didn't have a computer. So at nine o'clock that night, I drove to Kinko's, typed up a contract, and made ten copies on carbonless paper. (And yes, I realize that Criss Cross Directories, Kinko's, and carbonless paper all sound archaic. Those were the days, my friend.)

I was ready to go.

The next day, Mike and I went to the appointments together and sold to two out of the three customers for a total of about $17,000.

Man, this is a piece of cake, I thought. Then reality hit me. *Who's going to install the windows and siding we just sold?*

I was naive and excited, and I didn't even know all the questions I should be asking, but I was enthusiastic about the possibilities.

Doing quick calculations in my head, I figured I could sell $48,000 in a month. After paying for the supplies and installation crew, what was left would be more than enough to handle my family's monthly expenses, the small amount of debt we had, and our mortgage. That evening I went home confident that I could make this new business work, so confident that I told my wife she would be able to quit her job before too long. Deanna earned a decent salary as a paralegal, but with four kids in daycare, we would save money if she could stay home with them. More important to both of us, however, was the reality that our children would only be young for a short time, and we wanted to be the ones raising them and experiencing the daily milestones as they grew.

Deanna, who is much more even-keeled than me and had witnessed a number of my business startups and failures already, just smiled and said she thought it sounded like a good idea. What she didn't say (but was probably thinking) was, *Show me the money*. She never doubted my ability, but because she is cautious with our money, she took a wait-and-see approach.

I waited tables on Friday and Saturday nights for few months until we had some cashflow with the business. By that time, I had no doubt at all that Medina Exteriors was going to succeed, and a few months later, Deanna left her job.

You Don't Know What You Don't Know

I was flying high when I got home from those first three sales calls. Ideas, dreams, and possibilities raced through my mind. I'd been in business for roughly twenty-four hours, and all I could see was a bigger, brighter future.

During the past several years, I have learned so much about myself as an entrepreneur and a leader. What I can articulate now that I didn't have the words for when I started my company is that I'm a visionary who tends to leap before I look. In other words, I'm comfortable taking imperfect action. Any step forward is better than going nowhere or, worse, going backward.

It took me only seconds to agree to Mike's suggestion to start my own business. Within a couple of hours, I was on the phone with potential customers. And less than twenty-four hours later, I had made my first two sales.

While I was flying high on excitement and possibilities, I also felt like I was flying blind. I had no idea what to do first or what to do next, but it didn't seem to matter. I just took one step forward after another, and eventually, all those steps led to somewhere great.

The truth, though, is that, while there was so much I knew I didn't know—and so much more that I *didn't know* I didn't know— my business ventures, people skills, sales experience, and the personal learning I had pursued had all given me the confidence to make the leap.

- Having sold everything from life insurance to vacuums and gym memberships, I knew how to relate to the customers and understand their needs.
- Reading countless sales books equipped me to make the most of my unique ability, which is sales.

> **Unique Ability®**, by definition, is the essence of what you love to do and do best. It's your own set of natural talents and the passion that fuels you to contribute in the ways that most motivate you. When articulated, it describes the "you" that makes you who you are. —**Dan Sullivan, Strategic Coach**[6]

- I had sold windows and siding for someone else for several months, so I had some insight into the industry.
- I had a mentor, Mike, who was willing to walk beside me and help me get started.

My guess is that you, too, have a lot more working in your favor than you realize. You also probably have a lot to learn, just as I did and still do. You may not even know what questions you need to ask or where you're going to find the answers. That's okay. One imperfect step forward is all it takes to start (and keep) moving in the right direction.

Principle 3: Imperfect Action Pays Off

Four or five years after that first day, I did some more work for Alan Gordon, who had been one of my first two customers. When we reconnected, I mentioned to him that the first time we met had been on my first day in business.

"I would have never known," he replied.

Imperfect action fueled by confidence and a positive attitude will make that kind of impression. I didn't know what I was doing my first day on the job, but I didn't let it show.

My imperfect action paid off, and this first leap wouldn't be my last.

Through the years, I've used this principle of taking imperfect action to test all sorts of ideas, and because I know that failure is part of the entrepreneurial process (see chapter 2), I'm okay with making a move even when I haven't worked out all the details.

One recent example of taking an imperfect step forward is with our new software: Experts Made. The platform will be released in January 2023 and is a powerful tool for the kitchen and bath industry. Designers have to use a number of platforms (Excel, Word, CRMs, production software, etc.) on a daily basis, and each program comes with its own licensing fees and learning curves, which can make it difficult to train team members and scale efficiently. To help address these issues, we developed a single, industry-specific platform that streamlines the process and integrates all the tools and services designers need. Experts Made simplifies keeping track of clients' needs, orders, and designs. Beyond that, it makes it easy for designers to train their team members and scale their businesses while ensuring a consistent experience from client to client regardless of who handles the account.

Others had tried and failed to build a program like this. My team and I knew the flaws of the existing programs—for example, most were too generic to be helpful to our industry, and their limitations created bottlenecks in the workflow. Using what we knew, we took imperfect action and hired the best development team we could find to create the software we needed.

To learn more about Experts Made, scan the QR code or visit expertsmade.com.

When I first had the idea to create this software, I had no clue how to make it happen. I just knew that if I could take the processes we've developed at Medina Exteriors & Remodeling + Simply Distinct Kitchens and Baths and build a software around them, then it would transform our entire industry.

I didn't even know what questions to ask, but as I had done with Mike all those years ago, I found someone who had the expertise and could guide our team through the process. It's been exciting to create something that has the potential to help so many people, and watching it take shape and become a reality has been a thrill.

Imperfect action gets you started. You may end up needing to adjust or move in a slightly different direction, but at least you're up and running.

The enemy of taking imperfect action is analysis paralysis. Too many would-be businesses never grow beyond an idea because the person holding the seed of a dream can't imagine what the dream could look like fully grown. It's not uncommon for people to consider all the options, evaluate all the pros and cons, research ideas to death, and then never make the first move.

I've been taking imperfect action for thirty years now, and not once have I regretted it.

Application

- What imperfect action have you taken that has paid off?
- What is an area of your business where you're hesitant to move forward because you don't have all the answers?
- To whom can you reach out and ask for insight or guidance?

CHAPTER 4
NOT AS EASY AS I THOUGHT

An investment in knowledge pays the best interest.

—Benjamin Franklin

Medina Exteriors was up and running full steam. Those first two jobs gave me the confidence to set more appointments and make more sales. Selling was what I did best, and I loved that part of the job—in fact, I still do. Meeting with potential clients, uncovering their needs, and figuring out how best to serve them is my sweet spot.

If sales had been my only job, life would have been great. But over the next five years, I discovered that being an entrepreneur *wasn't* a piece of cake. Every day, I managed countless details to keep the company running. I had to order materials from vendors and pay the invoices. I had to hire subcontractors and pay them. Very often, I was out at the jobsite working side-by-side with the crew to install windows and siding or put on a new roof. Then there were payroll taxes to pay and forms to file.

And I did it all.

On the upside, the business was earning good money, which meant I no longer had to work a second job at a restaurant to pay the mortgage each month. Another benefit was that I controlled my schedule. I intentionally made time for my wife and our children, who ranged from newborn to six years old when the business launched. Even if it meant coming home for dinner and heading back out for an evening sales appointment, my family always came first.

The other downside was that, while I loved being in my sweet spot in sales and even enjoyed working on the jobs, I struggled with handling the books. The money came rolling in from Day One. The problem was, I didn't know what to do with it. I made orders and shuffled money from one invoice to the next, trying—and often failing—to remember who needed to be paid and when.

Within a year or so, the business was about $75,000 in debt because of overdue bills and taxes. We owed distributors for materials, and I had no idea—none—what I was doing when it came to payroll taxes.

I wasn't about to quit, though. My family was counting on me to make the business work. I dreaded the thought of telling my wife she had to go back to working in an office, so I worked harder, convinced I could outsell my problems.

It's Lonely at the Top

I had become an expert at taking imperfect action, but as I mentioned in the previous chapter, I didn't know what I didn't know. When the payroll taxes came due, it became painfully obvious that I needed some help. That *not knowing* was costing me time, money, and peace of mind.

Maybe you're in a similar spot.

It's common for entrepreneurs to launch as "solopreneurs." As the leader, they are the one with the vision and passion. They build a team or hire contractors as the business grows, but no one loves the company as much as the leader. The leader will do almost anything to succeed. If that means wearing all the hats and working extra hours, so be it. If it requires making decisions without having all the answers, then, so be it.

At some point, however, that way of working becomes unsustainable. You realize that you need help, but you aren't sure where to turn to find it. Everyone in your company is looking to *you* for leadership. They're expecting *you* to have the answers.

I didn't have the answers, but I knew they were out there. It was time for me to find them.

Principle 4: Be a Good Student

It's no secret that I disliked school. My grades in high school were decent enough, but so much of my time in the classroom felt useless and impractical. The same held true in college. But even though I wanted out of the classroom, I've always loved learning.

Even as a kid, I had a knack for learning new things. I'm observant and pick up on concepts quickly. I'm also able to take others' ideas and processes and adapt them to fit my personality and how I work best.

Five years into building the business, I realized that my company was like a bicycle wheel and I was the hub. The business was rolling quickly and moving in the right direction, but the wheel was wobbling all over the place. I needed to add spokes to give the wheel stability so it could roll straighter and more smoothly.

The spokes I needed were education.

- I needed input from people who were on a similar journey but had already been where I was.
- I needed to observe people working in businesses that were running well and efficiently.
- I needed people who would tell me what questions to ask and help me figure out what I didn't know.
- I needed to learn from people on the jobsites—roofers, siding experts, and window installers—so I really understood

the processes, needs, and time requirements for the products and services I sold.

I had so much to learn, and for the most part, I was ready. I knew there were other companies and contractors in my area that had a similar focus. Certainly, some would be willing to talk with me, but self-preservation often keeps people from sharing their best ideas. After all, no one wants to give company secrets away to the competition.

I knew I needed truth-tellers in my life—people who would look out for my best interests, point out my blind spots, and show me how to take the next leaps forward. In hopes of finding those people, I joined Proof Management, an industry networking group. It was a non-compete group, meaning I represented the only company like mine from my area. The membership fee felt a little steep at the time, but I believed the learning and collaboration that would come out of the group would be worth it in the long run.

Being part of that network helped me add some spokes to the wheel, and I came away from my first annual meeting with great insight and the motivation to work harder and smarter. But since it was a new venture for me, I didn't really know what to expect or how vulnerable I could be during that first year. While I asked questions and listened to others share, I wasn't ready to open up about all my struggles. Based on the little I was willing to reveal, the consensus from the group was that I needed to generate more income.

When I got home, my kids and I passed out fliers in the surrounding neighborhoods. I set appointment after appointment and ramped up our installation schedule. The income grew, but I was still handling the books and scheduling—and I was still struggling.

Humility Is Essential for Learning

Earlier I said that, *for the most part*, I was ready to learn. I knew I needed more information—more spokes—but pride kept me from telling my peers in the group exactly how much I owed or how much I hated keeping the books. On top of that, my ego had a habit of tricking me into thinking I knew more than I did.

Case in point: Because I was committed to learning, I had watched a few videos on how to roof. I felt pretty confident that I understood the process—or maybe I just thought I knew it all. *I mean, how hard could it be, right?*

Well, at the first annual meeting I attended with the networking group, I put my foot in my mouth in a big way. After sitting down next to a roofer named Bud, I got to talking, and eventually *arguing*, with him about roofing.

Bud told me that it took more time to lay some types of shingles than others.

Rather than asking why, I said, "No, it doesn't." After all, I'd watched the videos. "A shingle's a shingle. You just lay them down."

Because Bud was a truth-teller, he wasn't going to let me get away with prideful ignorance. Our conversation turned slightly confrontational as he explained the technical aspects of different types of shingles and why some do indeed require more time to install properly.

When he was done, I realized my mistake. I was a salesman telling a professional roof installer how to do his job. If the tables were turned and he had started telling me how easy it was to sell, I would have been just as irritated as he had been with me. Bud was a good sport about it, though, and I left the conversation having learned two things: 1) It takes longer to install some shingles than others, and 2) if you want to be a good student, you have to be humble enough to shut up and learn from the people who are willing to teach you.

Be a good student, a humble student. People will respect you more (and work harder for you) if you are willing to learn. When I applied this principle, the wheel straightened up, and we've been rolling smoothly now for thirty years.

Application

- What are you faking your way through? Get honest with yourself and get some help.
- From whom can you learn?
- Who is your mentor?

CHAPTER 5
NOW WE'RE ROLLING

As iron sharpens iron, so one person sharpens another.

—Proverbs 27:17, NIV

I returned to the networking group's annual meeting for the third consecutive year. The group had been fantastic. I had learned so much—mostly about how much more I needed to learn. I'd found a few like-minded guys who had become good friends. I could call with questions or to bounce ideas off them, and they felt free to do the same with me.

As for the business, our sales were great, but my stress level was off the charts. I was still trying to manage the books and wear all the hats, and every year, the company owed even more. The business was now $100,000 in the red, and I'd become a master at beating myself up. *How could our sales be so good and our debt be so high?*

Walking into the meeting that year, I felt defeated and depressed. The two previous years, I had kept up my guard, learning and sharing more each year, but never being completely transparent. That year, however, I couldn't hide the stress I felt. It literally weighed my shoulders down. People noticed it in the way I carried myself. They saw it on my face.

When Mark told me I looked like I had the weight of the world on my shoulders, I felt a crack streak up the dam that had held my emotions in check for so long. I had no one in my company in whom I could confide—they were all looking to me for leadership. My wife had four kids to wrangle and a household to manage, so I didn't want to burden her with the details of day-to-day operations. The guys in my networking group were the closest thing I had to confidants, but so far, I hadn't been willing to talk openly with them about how bad things really were.

Throughout the meeting, the pressure continued to build until, finally, the dam burst when Monroe called me out on my less-than-brilliant idea to try to figure everything out on my own. The blessing of that networking group was that it surrounded me with truth-tellers like Bud, Monroe, Kevin, Kinney, and others who called BS on my faulty mindset—a mindset that said I had to do everything myself. It was an approach that had worked for me most of my life, but with the company pushing against my capabilities in terms of both skill and time, I needed to rethink the way I ran the business.

I knew I had hit rock bottom when I accidentally walked into the coat closet trying to escape the embarrassment of losing it in front of a room full of guys I respected. (You'll remember that story from the introduction of this book.)

From the moment I stepped out of that closet, I set all pretense and bravado aside. I was broken and finally ready to do whatever I needed to do. My current pace simply wasn't sustainable.

Monroe and Bud found a place for us to talk and asked Kevin and Kinney, a couple of the guys I'd gotten to know well and trusted, to join us. I told them everything. I admitted that I had no business keeping the books and offered the debt and overdue bills as proof. I felt like the company was on life support and that, at any minute, someone would pull the plug, but I had worked so hard for so long trying to do it all myself that I couldn't see any other options.

Thankfully, the members of my networking group had some ideas. Now that they finally had the full picture, they could clearly see the solution wasn't simply to work harder and sell more. Doing the same thing I had been doing wasn't going to change anything, so we worked out a two-year plan for how to eliminate the debt. The plan had two basic parts:

First, I had to stop doing the books. After some thought, discussion, and prayer, Deanna agreed to take over the financial side of the business. She had the mind and skills necessary for keeping up with numbers, taxes, and all the details that slipped by me.

Second, to get more money to funnel to the bottom line, I would act as foreman on the jobs. Previously, I had hired subcontractors as foremen. With me working as the foreman, that pay would drop to the bottom line, thus accelerating our debt reduction.

I left that year's annual meeting recharged and excited about the future of our company. With a clear plan in place, my stress level dropped immediately.

It wasn't necessarily easy for me to hand over the books to my wife. I was used to being responsible for and in control of everything, so I kept trying to manage the finances by looking over her shoulder, and to be honest, I was making a mess of things.

Finally, Deanna told me, "I'm only going to do this if you let me have the books 100 percent." I agreed to step back and focus on my area of expertise so she could do the same. To keep me accountable to the plan, Monroe, Bud, and my friend Kevin agreed to be the muscle, so to speak. If and when I stepped out of my lane into hers by trying to take over or meddle with the books, Deanna knew she could call one of those guys to get me back on course.

It only happened a couple of times, and when it did, whoever she called would reach out to me and hold me accountable to the plan we had developed together. They reminded me why the plan would work—and why me trying to control everything *wouldn't*.

That third annual meeting was in the fall of 2002, and by May of 2004, Deanna had the company out of debt. Twenty-two months was all it took—twenty-two months that included a closet-crisis moment, humility, a willingness to learn, and a network of truth-tellers.

Like It or Not, Entrepreneurs Need Support

Where are you in your business? Are things going the way you want—the way you'd envisioned when you dreamed of starting a company? Or are you where I was: still trying to do it all yourself?

If you are an entrepreneur, then you need support. We all do! Even though you are at the top of the accountability chart, you aren't responsible for performing every task. I know that's how it might seem, especially in the beginning. The larger your company grows, however, the more essential it becomes to create a workable plan that allows you to maximize your unique abilities and step away from roles that don't fit your gifts or personality style.

It can be hard to create that plan on your own. You're so close to the business and so entrenched in every aspect, you may not be able to see what you need to change. Like-minded entrepreneurs, like those I found in my networking group, can help you identify the weak spots and find ways to shore them up.

During those first few years in business, my learning curve was like Mt. Everest because every aspect involved on-the-job training. Sure, I brought my unique abilities with me, just like you do. Sales and customers service were two things I knew I could do well right from the beginning. Everything else, though, required that I learn something new, and for several years, I learned by trial and error.

If that's where you are, then you are probably working a lot harder than you have to. Putting in sixty to seventy hours a week may work for a while, but it's not a way to live long-term.

Principle 5: Network and Apply What You Learn

It had taken me three years to get to the point where I was willing to listen and learn with humility. When I got honest with myself and transparent with the guys in my networking group, my learning curve went from a relentless, steep, uphill climb to a trek that was much more manageable and enjoyable. The more I learned and applied others' hard-won insight and experience, the faster and more efficiently our company grew.

When I got home from that third annual meeting, Deanna and I scheduled visits with office managers and bookkeepers at companies from the networking group that were similar in size to Medina Exteriors. Like our business, those companies had one salesperson and someone to do the books and serve as office manager. They showed Deanna their processes for keeping inventory, making orders, paying contractors, vendors, and taxes.

She took what she learned and got the financial side of our business working more efficiently than it ever had before. Today, she still serves as the CFO of Medina Exteriors & Remodeling + Kitchens and Baths, and we've hired a dedicated office manager so Deanna can focus her time in the area of her unique ability.

Find Your Tribe(s)

The relationships that come out of good networking groups are invaluable. Before I joined mine, I had never experienced the benefits of having accountability in business. The group provided a community that created unique value for each of us, and because of the non-compete criteria for membership, everyone could be open without worrying someone would steal their ideas.

The networking group had forty-eight total members, and we met in smaller groups of twelve. Within the smaller groups, people typically found three or four people with whom they really connected. For me, it was Bud, Kevin, and Kinney. They have businesses similar to mine, but they live in different states and all have different skills. Kevin and I both excel in sales, so we sharpen one another by listening to the other's pitches and role-playing scenarios over the phone. Kinney is more of a technician, though, so I am able to help him with sales, and he has helped me better understand building and installation techniques and provided insight on vendors and materials.

To this day, we're all still great friends. We *get* each other. I know that when I'm having an issue, or I have a crazy idea for marketing, or I'm wondering about a new vendor, I can pick up the phone or send an email and get their insight and honest feedback. That's something I didn't have when I was going it alone.

A few years ago, I started learning from Dan Sullivan and his Strategic Coach© organization, where I found other entrepreneurs in all sorts of industries who were focused on building more efficient and profitable businesses. Medina Exteriors then joined EOS (Entrepreneurial Operating System) Worldwide®, where in addition to getting a framework that helps my business run more effectively, I've connected with other business leaders who have become friends and mentors.

Surround yourself with truth-tellers: people who care about you and want to see you succeed, people to whom you feel accountable and who feel accountable to you, people you trust. Your network is critical to your success as an entrepreneurial leader.

Application

- What networking groups serve your industry? Are you a member of any of them?
- Where could you find like-minded people to learn from and with?
- Who are the truth-tellers in your life?

CHAPTER 6
INTO THE FIELD WE GO

I don't know of any entrepreneurs who have achieved any level of success without persistence and determination.

—Harvey Mackay

"Okay, what's next?" I asked.

From the top of the house, my cell phone got great reception. Looking down, I smiled at the discarded shingles, evidence of the work that had already transpired that spring morning.

The plan to get the company into the black included me learning how to roof. I had sold roofs for years, but talking about installation was different than doing it. Even though I had watched my subcontractors install roofs on countless residential properties, I had never done the actual work. If I could learn the trade, then the money I would have paid a foreman for a roofing project would go directly to our bottom line.

I got home from that networking meeting and immediately started watching roofing videos. To get hands-on experience, I spent two weeks training under Bud. (Yes, this was the same Bud I had so confidently and ignorantly told "a shingle's a shingle" at that first annual meeting. Thankfully, he didn't hold it against me.)

Bud and his wife generously allowed me to stay at their home, and in return for room and board, I roofed right alongside Bud for two weeks to learn the mechanics of roofing.

Armed with video training and some hands-on experience, it was time for me to do my first roof. I had sold a roof and hired a guy to help me, and I was ready to get started.

Then I called Bud.

"How do I start?" I asked.

"Go up there and tear off the roof, and then call me back," he told me.

When we had torn off the old shingles, I called Bud back. "Okay, what's next?"

And so it went throughout the next couple of days as Bud instructed me on each step of the process—all over the phone.

Roofing was hard, physical labor, but it was worth it to know the company's profits would increase with each job I took on as foreman. Learning the installation side of the business also built up my confidence. I knew sales was my unique ability, and I had no intention of wearing both hats forever, but learning the process firsthand gave me new insight into the business and ended up giving me more credibility with my subcontractors and team members down the road.

While I was sweating outdoors, my wife was hard at work in our home office getting the company's books in order. I had relinquished control of the finances to Deanna, and she had found her own unique ability as a result. Her detail-focused personality fit perfectly with her new role in the company. Within a matter of months, she had efficient processes in place to ensure our taxes, vendors, and subcontractors were paid on time. In less than two years, she had us completely out of debt.

We had climbed from a pit of despair to a place where I, as the visionary for the company, could once again see new and bigger possibilities. And it felt good.

Failure Stings

For years, it felt like I had to learn everything twice—once the wrong way and then once the right way. What I learned from those experiences was that when you take imperfect action, you'll have plenty of opportunities for do-overs.

Failure is part of the entrepreneurial experience. In fact, I believe that if you fail to fail, you're still failing because you aren't learning, growing, and trying new things. But knowing that failure is normal still doesn't take the sting out of it.

No one enjoys failing, which is why one of the principles of imperfect action is learning to fail *fast*. The less time you spend flailing about trying to figure out what to do next or what to do differently, the more quickly you can start moving in the right direction again.

Once I found the networking group, I discovered that my learning didn't have to come from my mistakes alone. I also could learn from the experiences of people who had been where I wanted to go. In some cases, their knowledge helped me avoid costly mistakes. In other cases, what I gleaned from others allowed me to minimize the time it took to recover from a misstep.

Principle 6: Do Whatever It Takes to Survive, Persevere, and Succeed

The alternative to learning from failure was to quit, and I wasn't about to give up. By this time, I had invested almost ten years of my life in building the business. For all the stress I had endured and mistakes I had made, I loved my work. I loved knowing that I was making a difference in people's lives by helping them make their homes more beautiful and energy-efficient.

There was no way I was going to quit.

In chapter 2, I told you that I ran through a series of false starts before starting Medina Exteriors. I tried a variety of business models on for size, but every time, within six months or so, I would know something wasn't right. Either the passion wasn't there or something about the work just didn't fit me, my personality, my unique ability, or my lifestyle as a husband and father. In each of those scenarios, it was easy to quit. I thought of those ventures as experiments. They were fruitful failures in that I earned income for my family and, equally as important, learned about myself in the process.

Persevering in any of those business opportunities would only have prolonged the inevitable. They weren't a fit, and I knew it. It was good and right for me to quit each of those endeavors as soon as that truth became clear.

This time, it was different. For this business, perseverance was the only option.

Perseverance, or the lack thereof, is often what makes or breaks a company. Steve Jobs put it this way: "I'm convinced that about half of what separates the successful entrepreneurs from the non-successful ones is pure perseverance. It is so hard, and you pour so much of your life into this thing, there are such rough moments in time that most people give up. And I don't blame them, it's really tough."[7]

Your willingness to persevere comes down to one question: Are you an entrepreneur, or not? Entrepreneurs expect things to go right because they have a positive mindset, and that same mindset allows them to see failure as an opportunity for growth.

Most people, however, don't view failure through that lens. They see it as demoralizing and defeating, and let's be honest, sometimes it is. But if you are an entrepreneur and are passionate about the mission of your company and the value you bring to the world, then you don't quit. You do whatever it takes to survive and succeed.

That's what I was doing when I learned how to roof. I didn't want to be a roofer for life. What I wanted was for my company to get out of debt so we could grow. I wanted Medina Exteriors to succeed. And if that meant putting in a little—or a lot—of sweat equity, then so be it. I worked on the jobsites during the day and made my sales calls at night.

A few years later, I learned how to install siding and windows the same way I had learned how to roof: through videos and hands-on experience. In this case, my decision to go into the field wasn't about getting out of debt (since Deanna was already a master at keeping the company in the black). I did it so we could expand the business. I hired a foreman to work the roofing jobs, and I worked the siding jobs. Little by little, we were able to scale and hire more people, help more homeowners, and enjoy higher profits. I eventually hired a foreman so I could focus on growing other areas of the business, but I'm always ready to get back in the field if I need to.

Are You Endangering Your Survival?

Perseverance and success require as much mental work as they do physical labor. It is no problem for me to roll up my sleeves when times get tough. The threat of extinction heightens my will to survive, so if there's a choice between fight or flight, I'm going to fight every time. That's my nature.

Sometimes, however, entrepreneurs endanger their business's survival by setting themselves up for failure. They engage in self-sabotage, but it's rarely a conscious decision. Procrastination on making calls, for example, can put you behind in reaching your sales goal. Or maybe you invest more than you should in equipment, which increases your expenses, so you've got to do more work to make sure you can pay the bill when it comes due.

Self-sabotage is not limited to your business goals. It happens in a thousand different ways in all areas of life—from relationships, to sobriety, to diet, to spending habits. The root cause in most cases is a lack of self-esteem or self-belief, and because we rarely realize what we're doing, we may not stop until someone else points out the pattern.

For years, I didn't believe I was successful. I was just doing my thing, and I didn't think of it as anything special. When you build a business from the ground up and hit those anniversary marks—one year, three years, five years, and so on—it is a great achievement. In my mind, though, I wasn't successful yet, even though our company was producing steady profit, happy team members, and satisfied customers.

One way I used to sabotage myself was to back myself into a corner. Looking back, I can see that I did certain things—like take on debt—because it gave me something to fight against, and it felt good when I won. The thing is, I didn't realize what I was doing.

One day Kevin, my friend from the networking group, commented, "It seems like you're always fighting from the back, coming from behind to save the day."

"You know me, man," I said. "I'm the champion. I won't stop fighting until I get out of that corner."

Kevin looked at me and asked, "Brett, what if you were to start from the front, like running a marathon? What if you took all that energy you use to start from the back and used it to go from the front forward instead?"

For some reason, I had never thought of success like that, but looking at it that way, I realized success didn't have to be a fight or a struggle. That conversation shifted my mindset. I started believing in myself and recognizing my success, and I stopped doing things that endangered my business's survival.

Perseverance requires work. It requires a commitment to do whatever it takes to survive and succeed. And sometimes it starts with changing the way you think about yourself.

Application

- Do you have the grit it takes to persevere?
- What short-term sacrifices could you make to ensure the growth or health of your company?
- What changes could help your business be more profitable?
- What successes have you already experienced?

CHAPTER 7
THE EVOLUTION OF A COMPANY'S CULTURE

Culture eats strategy for breakfast.

—Peter Drucker

Our first employment ad in the newspaper read, "Help Wanted: Get Down and Dirty Working with Your Hands."

One-hundred-and-fifty people applied.

This was right during the time I was running myself into the ground trying to do everything on my own. I needed a lead, someone I could trust to work onsite with the first roofing and siding crews we had hired. (Prior to having our own crews, we used subcontractors for the projects.)

I interviewed a few people from the 150 applicants and picked someone to fill the lead spot.

At the time, we didn't have any kind of protocol for hiring—no drug testing or clear wage structure—but we had developed clear processes for each type of install project. The crews just plugged into the project and followed the process. That part worked well enough and ensured the quality of work I wanted for our customers.

The problem was that the crew members, and even the lead, didn't understand what kind of company I wanted ours to be or the culture I wanted to create. They didn't understand because I hadn't told them. I had made my expectations about efficiency and meeting deadlines clear, and I thought that was enough. It wasn't long before I realized there was so much more to leading people well. Building the culture of our company was about more than profits and efficiencies. I wanted to improve people's lives—from our customers to our team members. Without clear guidelines, I realized, the people we had hired would never succeed with our company.

We kept growing, and about two years after placing that first employment ad, I needed another lead. I put the same advertisement in the paper but added three words: "drug-free company." That time, only a handful of people applied, and none of them were qualified for the job.

Rather than hiring someone else who wasn't a fit, we continued with our foreman overseeing the roofing crew and me working as the foreman for the siding crew, again ignoring the red flags warning me to be a better leader.

Then one day I was working on a jobsite with the roofing crew when the foreman fell off the roof. Despite my urging, he refused to go to the hospital. What I didn't know then was that he was high on cocaine and wanted to avoid any kind of investigation. When I learned the truth, I had no choice but to fire him on the spot.

Without a roofing foreman, we were back to using subcontractors to fill that role. I worked on small jobs and repairs and focused on sales.

During that time, I also reassessed our hiring practices and how we could improve them to create a positive culture throughout our company. I had taken an *E-Myth Revisited* course and learned how to serve and manage better not only the business but also the teams we hired. I tapped into the power of my networking group, too, and adapted some ideas that had worked for others.

One principle I learned from a painter in the networking group continues to serve me well when we have an opening to fill: It's human nature for people to overstate their value in an interview. People often exaggerate their skill level in hopes of being hired at a higher rate, so we set up a process that allows us to assess how qualified they really are for the job. We tell applicants to come to their interview in work clothes, and we begin by asking open-ended questions, including questions about their skill level and the hourly rate they believe they're worth. If applicants pass the question phase of the interview, we move to the real-world trial. We have a workstation set up in the warehouse where applicants are given an hour to install a product. I watch them work and then inspect the finished product.

The system works beautifully because it does one of three things:

- It shows me that the applicant doesn't have the required skills.

- It lets me know if they have potential but need some training, which gives me a feel for an appropriate pay level. If they need improvement but are a cultural fit, I offer them a lower pay rate and train them up to the point that they are qualified to earn the higher rate they wanted.

- It shows me they have what it takes. They can walk the talk and do what they said they could.

Using this hiring method, I no longer have to wonder if the applicant can actually do the job. The proof is in their work.

With clear expectations in place, we started hiring again. Once we established the team, I made sure they were in roles where they could perform in their unique ability (although I didn't use that phrase until I heard Dan Sullivan explain it years later). I don't micromanage them. When someone makes a mistake, either I or their lead will address it with them. I set the expectation that everyone will correct and learn from their mistakes, and that includes me.

As a teenager, I spent a couple of summers laying brick for a company that belonged to a friend of my dad. We worked in the basements of new builds laying cinder blocks for the foundation. I was young and green, but I was strong and could work quickly—never quickly enough, though. It didn't matter how many bricks I laid or how clean the work was, the lead for the team would cuss a blue streak at me almost every day. The idea on that crew was that you had to earn your stripes (by getting chewed out daily) before you could be treated with any kind of respect.

When I started my company, I knew that wasn't how I wanted to treat people, and my mentor Mike assured me that my company could be an exception to the norm in the construction industry. When people make mistakes, we talk with them about it. Tirades and foul language aren't part of the culture at our company, and that's by design.

One of the guys I hired on that second round of crews told me one day that the idea of learning and growing from mistakes was foreign in our industry. In every other place he'd worked, mistakes were met with a tirade of profanities. When he told me that, I knew the culture we had created was something special.

Good People Are Hard to Find

The three main aspects of business in this industry are operations, sales, and finances. As the leader, you need to know about all three of these areas, but you probably only need to be very good at one of them. The goal is for you to work in the area where you thrive and bring the most value to the business and to hire the right people to oversee and run the other areas.

Finding those people and managing them well isn't always easy. Creating a culture that makes people feel valued and where each person can use his or her unique ability on a regular basis requires intentionality on your part. For example, you might hire someone with the expectation that he'll do well in sales only to discover that operations is really where his strength lies. If he brings value to the team, then you'll figure out how to readjust his expectations and roles because you know that good people—people who care about the customers and the success of the company instead of just their paychecks—can be hard to find.

You will also have to fight the temptation to hire *anybody* when you have more work than you can handle. You might get desperate and think, *It doesn't matter who—I just need someone to fill the role.* If the person you hire isn't the right fit for the culture you're building, however, you'll soon know it, and you'll then be left with two choices: fire the person, or hope that he or she quits while the rest of the team suffers in the meantime. (Incidentally, if I'm in that position, I'm going to cut my losses. In the end, it's a better choice for everyone, even the person who gets fired.)

Principal 7: Be Willing to Make Changes

When our company joined EOS Worldwide®, we put words to the kind of culture we wanted. We set up accountability charts and put our core values on paper. Seeing our values in black and white reaffirmed that we had a unique approach and culture for a construction company. We had been living our core values for years, but putting them on paper reinforced our belief in who we were and the kind of people we would hire and keep on the team. (I've included our core values at the end of the chapter.)

In addition, we identified our purpose and passion as "Improving Lives by Improving Homes." Having the words to clearly state our driving motivation (notice that it isn't money) unified our team with a clear, shared mission.

One simple example of how that mission plays out makes me really proud of our team and the culture we've developed. A few winters ago, we had a kitchen remodel in the works at an elderly couple's house. A storm came through and dumped two feet of snow on the town and completely blocked their driveway. I sent a note to the couple to reschedule the work, explaining that the trucks couldn't make it up the driveway.

The reply came back, "We'll make sure we shovel the driveway this weekend."

"Great, thank you very much," I typed before signing off.

A minute later, the project manager and our master carpenter, Kevin, called me. He'd seen the thread of messages.

"You know," he said. "I'm not sure 'improving lives by improving homes' means allowing an elderly couple to shovel two feet of slushy snow so we can be there on Monday."

"You're right," I said. And he was. I called a couple of buddies who plowed the driveway for them. I sent the clients a note to let them know they didn't have to worry about shoveling snow and that there would be no charge for plowing it for them. I also gave Kevin the credit. Needless to say, the clients were blown away by that kind of customer service.

Even Difficult Changes Can Be Good

Knowing what's important to you also allows you to identify the people who don't fit the culture. I had a lead working for me for a couple of years who didn't buy into our culture. Nobody I put with him on a job wanted to keep working with him. His attitude toward the crew members left a lot to be desired, and after a few people asked me to move them to other jobs, it was clear to me he was the problem.

I didn't want to make a rushed decision, and honestly, I needed someone in that role. I knew I needed a better handle on the situation, so I began making frequent stops at his jobsites to check in. In addition to his bad attitude toward the crew, I also often found him taking a company-sponsored break. Rather than the eight hours a day I was paying him for, he probably only worked between four and five hours.

I asked him to come to my office to talk. The first thing he told me when he sat down was that he wanted a raise. Rather than fire him on the spot, which would have put us in a bind, I gave him the opportunity to make some changes. I clearly explained my expectations, both in terms of work ethic and the way he interacted with the crew. If he was willing operate in line with our culture, then he could stay, and only *then* would we talk about a raise.

Several months later, he was back in my office. He hadn't changed. When I laid out the evidence that he hadn't met the expectations, he didn't disagree. I half-expected him to blow up at me when I told him we had to let him go, but he didn't. He couldn't argue with the facts, and he knew it.

We've intentionally centered our company's culture on character and integrity. People know we're going to pay them fairly and that we won't do anything under the table. We are committed to doing business in a way that is honest—from the taxes we pay to our willingness to fix mistakes—even if the client doesn't know or can't tell that something isn't right. We do that because: 1) it's the right thing to do, 2) it builds the business on a strong foundation, and 3) it encourages team members to become personally invested in the success of the company.

When you allow people to work in their unique ability, treat them with respect, and make your expectations clear, you create a place where people want to work. More than that, your people will work harder for you because they know you care. When that happens, you cross the threshold from an owner-run company, where you oversee every detail, to a self-managed company, where your team members take on an entrepreneurial mindset because they love the company almost as much as you do.

Our Core Values

Character
- Be humbly confident.
- Be honest with yourself and open with the team.
- Be accountable to one another.
- Find joy in others' successes.

Optimism
- Come to work with an open mind.
- Have a healthy, positive attitude.
- Be a great team player.
- Contribute to a healthy, positive culture.

Readiness
- Be organized.
- Have a forward-thinking mindset. Be proactive and prepared.
- Stay focused on the task.
- Keep a positive outlook and be ready to problem-solve.

Evolution
- Be open-minded about change.
- Be flexible.
- Be hungry to grow professionally and personally.
- Listen to clients and each other to continually improve products, training, and client and team experiences.
- Learn, share, stumble, succeed, and grow.

Application

- What are your company's core values?
- Who on your team would fit better in a different role?
- Is there anyone you need to fire?

CHAPTER 8
BECOMING A SELF-MANAGED BUSINESS

*Your past is important, but not nearly as important
as how you see your future.*

—**Zig Ziglar**

Processes became essential when we started climbing out of debt. With a finite number of hours in the day, I was only able to manage so much on my own. The greater the volume of jobs we had in the works at any one time, the more difficult it was for me to keep everything running smoothly.

Every organization has its tipping point, and I knew we had hit ours when finding the right people and developing clear processes became more important to me than managing all the details myself. It was difficult for me to loosen the grip I had as a leader, but I knew that if I wasn't willing to evolve, then the business would never become a self-managed organization.

The problem was, I didn't know what letting go looked like for me or the company. Being a student of sales and business, I had read books by Zig Ziglar, Dale Carnegie, and other master trainers who talked about developing systems to increase success. I knew I couldn't be everywhere at once and that I didn't want to work in the field forever. If the company was going to thrive, then everyone needed to be maximizing their unique ability, including me. The best way for me to improve the bottom line was to focus on selling. The McDonald's franchise fascinated me, and like the McDonald brothers had done, I wanted to create a turn-key business that offered a quality and consistent experience for customers regardless of who was serving them.

That's where processes came in.

As we grew, it was our processes for hiring, training, and doing installs that kept us moving forward. We documented everything and made sure everyone was on the same page. With the steps outlined, a lead could oversee a project with any crew. A clear and effective hiring process made it easier to find the right people, people who meshed well with the company's culture and believed in our mission to improve lives by improving homes. Intentionality in training helped us ensure quality work and consistent, positive experiences for our customers.

It was while I was in the field roofing that I began to grasp the potential for exponential growth. I realized I could cover our bottom-line expenses by running one crew. I started thinking that, by following consistent processes, if I could duplicate a crew, then another, and another, we could significantly increase our income and profit margins. We could follow the McDonald's model, just without the fries.

Having multiple crews in the field at once not only allowed us to do more jobs but also made us more competitive in our market. The key was finding our break-even point, the point at which costs and revenue were equal. Anything that came in beyond that would be pure profit.

Are You Working *on* Your Business or *in* Your Business?

One of the lessons I learned from Michael Gerber's *E-Myth Revisited* course was that I needed to be working on my business rather than in my business. I later learned from EOS® that being able to make that shift would require that the business be self-managed rather than owner-managed. That was the only way we were going to be able to grow the way I'd dreamed we would. It was also the only way I would be able to experience the abundance and freedom of time I'd imagined.

When I started the business, it was almost impossible to see how I could ever stop working *in* my business. I was it! Sure, I subcontracted crews to do the installs, but that came with its own issues. Sometimes a subcontractor would further subcontract the job, which made communication difficult. It was a little like the telephone game kids play: You started with one message and just hoped it made it all the way through to the person actually doing the work.

Then we started hiring crews of our own, which worked well once we got our hiring and training processes in place. I found that I could oversee four or five crews and still sell, but any more than that was too much. I had a choice: I could hire help, or I could limit the company's growth. Guess which one I chose?

What about you? Are you working on your business or in your business? Do you know how to make the shift from the former to the latter?

Principle 8: Learn, Collaborate, and Grow

Wanting or needing your business to be self-managed and knowing how to make that happen are two different things. Because I wanted to create a business that could run without me if necessary, I knew we needed processes for everyone to follow.

I found support and tools from a variety of places. First, within my non-compete networking group, I found people who were willing to share their best practices for training. Our team would visit these businesses and observe how they operated. It was one of the most powerful ways for us to learn because it let us see what worked and why. We offered the same opportunity for others in the group to learn from us, knowing that with an abundance mentality, we could help each other become better in all areas.

Through networking programs like Proof Management, Strategic Coach, and EOS®, as well as ongoing professional education from books and courses aimed at specific areas of business, I learned how to be strategic and systematize operations. It takes time and intentionality to map out a plan for the future, identify processes, and train people, but it's worth it.

When you have the right people in the right roles (where they can perform in their unique abilities) and you have the processes and technology to support them, you develop synergy as an organization. Everything starts to click into place, and you, as the leader, can finally experience the kind of financial and time freedom you've dreamed of since Day One.

Which brings me to the third tool that helped us operate efficiently within the processes we'd developed: technology. I told you that when I made those first three sales appointments, I didn't even own a computer. (At the time, mobile phones were the size of shoe boxes and cost forty-five cents a minute to use. I didn't own one of those either.) Today, I can't imagine not having a computer and a smartphone. We use technology for just about every aspect of the business. From our CRM to our inter-office communication to the tools we use for invoicing, paying, ordering, and tracking progress, technology keeps our company operating smoothly. And as I mentioned in Chapter 3, after being frustrated by the limitations of other programs and trying to piece together multiple platforms, I decided to design our Experts Made software specifically for the kitchen and bath design industry.

You may not need to go to the level of designing your own software, but regardless of what technology you use, I encourage you to evaluate it and see if it is working well for your team. Do the programs still serve your needs, or have you outgrown their capabilities? Do your team members know how to make the most of the platforms or programs?

New technologies come along every day that can simplify your life and your work. As your company grows and your needs change, be willing to explore your options and find what works best for your team members and the people you serve.

Determine What Processes You Need

Hiring
- Write job descriptions for everyone currently working in the company (including the owner).
- Write job descriptions for new roles you'd like to create or fill.
- Develop a company manual or handbook to set clear expectations.
- Identify your non-negotiables (e.g., drug-free work environment).
- Establish your Core Values, Mission, and/or Purpose Statement.

Training

Document the ideal process for each area of business and for each person's role, then train to those processes. I've identified a few areas where training is important in our business—your needs will be unique to your business. Clarify your best practices and decide how to train people on your processes and the technology or other tools that will equip them to succeed. While you're at it, decide who will do the training.

Bookkeeping—Invoicing, payments to vendors, contractors, and team members, and paying taxes

Office Management—Onboarding new clients, scheduling, assignments, human resources

Operations—Steps for how to deliver with excellence each product or service you provide

Sales—Scripts, role play, shadowing, evaluation of calls, how to make appointments, how to submit new orders or contracts

Find Your Break-Even Point and Scale

Okay, it's time to nerd out a little on numbers. You already know that numbers weren't my thing for a long time and that I no longer manage our books. It may not be your area of expertise either, but knowing your break-even point is eye-opening. Even if you find financial talk boring, stay with me here. I promise it'll be worth your time.

Finding your break-even point requires some reverse engineering. Start by tallying all your fixed or regular expenses for the year (salaries, overhead, equipment, etc.), then divide that by how many hours you and your team work in a year.

If, for example, you have a three-man crew and each person works forty hours a week fifty weeks of the year, then your annual hours will look like this:

2,000 hours X 3 team members = 6,000 hours

If your expenses are $300,000, then you need to charge $50 per hour for labor to break even. (Remember, you'll charge for supplies and shipping separately.)

$300,000 / 6,000 hours = $50 per hour for labor. That's your break-even point. If you bring in that much, then all your bills are paid, but there's zero profit for the company.

If 6,000 hours was the maximum you could work, then your best option for bringing in more profit would be to charge more for labor. If you increased to $55 per hour for labor, then the company would make a profit (income over and above your expenses) of $30,000.

$$6,000 \text{ hours} \times \$55 = \$330,000$$

That's great, but there's only so much clients are willing to pay, and you don't want to price yourself out of the market. The alternative to raising prices too high or too quickly is to scale. Adding more people, or, as in my company's case, another crew, to your team will raise your bottom-line expenses (more salaries to pay, another company vehicle, etc.), but it will also raise your profits.

For this example, let's say that hiring a second crew increases your expenses to $400,500. If your new crew is working forty hours a week, then you've doubled the company's annual hours for a total of 12,000 hours. If your labor charge is $50 per hour, then the company's profit would jump to $150,000.

$$12,000 \text{ hours} \times \$50 = \$600,000$$
$$\$600,000 - \$400,500 = \$150,000 \text{ profit}$$

In my role, I could oversee four or five crews at a time. Each crew I brought on increased the amount we paid in salaries, and I had to buy a few more trucks, but our other expenses stayed about the same.

Following this scenario, if I had five crews, then my expenses might be $1,030,000, but with 30,000 labor hours, the income would be $1,500,000. That's a profit for the company of $470,000 to use for upgrading equipment, marketing, or even raises.

$$30,000 \times 50 = \$1,500,000$$
$$\$1,500,000 - \$1,030,000 = \$470,000 \text{ profit}$$

I'm using hypothetical numbers to illustrate how to scale by increasing your team, but you can use the same math to find your break-even point and maximize your profits.

Of course, at some point, you'll hit a spot where overhead costs will need to increase significantly if you want to reach the next level of growth. You might, for example, need to hire another salesperson or buy a larger building to serve your company's needs. Anticipating this growth point and knowing your numbers prepares you to make an educated decision about your next steps. When you hit this point, the company may experience some growing pains. Profits will level out or even dip when and if you decide to do what's necessary to grow. But if you continue to scale, then after a year or two, the company's profits will increase.

Each time you hit a new growth point, rinse and repeat. It's a repeatable, sustainable process.

With this model, we were able to develop a strong brand in our area and expand to kitchen and bath remodeling. Scalability comes down to knowing your numbers and watching the bottom line as you hire more help.

One last note about scaling: I encourage you to let the process play out organically. There's no sense in hiring team members if you don't have regular work for them.

Create a Turn-Key Business

One benefit to creating processes and training people well is that it allows you to have a turn-key business. It equips the company to grow—to expand your brand, capacity, competitiveness, and profit—and become self-managed. That growth allows you to invest in others and provide opportunities for your team members to move up if they choose.

Another reason I wanted to create a turn-key business is so I can retire someday. With all the systems we have in place, I am confident that someone who has been trained through the company can one day manage the day-to-day operations without me. Alternatively, it opens the door for someone with a similar passion to buy the company from me and run the processes and systems that are already in place.

For now, though, knowing I can trust my team and the processes and technology we've developed allows me to spend more time using my unique ability and planning for our next move.

Application

- What processes do you need to define "on paper?"
- Who is responsible for training people in each area of your business?
- What is your break-even point?
- Whom do you need to hire?
- If you can't afford (or don't want) to hire a full-time team member, then are there ways you could use virtual assistants, freelancers, or subcontractors to expand your business, increase your profits, and improve your competitive edge?

CHAPTER 9
GET BACK UP (AGAIN)

You may not realize it when it happens, but a kick in the teeth may be the best thing in the world for you.

—Walt Disney

Monday, March 30, 2020, was brutal. A week earlier, Ohio had issued an official stay-at-home order, bringing all work to a screeching halt. We had been through rough times before, but nothing was worse than having to lay off all our team members.

As an entrepreneur, you want to take care of your team. Your drive is to help people grow and succeed. Closing the doors for an undetermined, unknowable length of time seemed unimaginable, but that's exactly what happened to our company and hundreds of thousands of others.

Deanna and I had evaluated all available options. I had met with a few business mentors and spiritual leaders. After difficult deliberation and much prayer, I decided to temporarily shut down the company. It was a gut-wrenching decision, but I believed it was the right one. If there was going to be a company to come back to, we had to lay off everyone. We hoped for the best—that the shutdown would only last a week or two—but we had no idea what would happen. Our people understood, and they were able to get unemployment to compensate for the loss of income, but that didn't make it any easier to deliver the news.

Then, on the night of April 7, 2020, an F1 tornado ripped through our county. On April 8, my project manager and I got to work. We went from full stop to full speed overnight. Over the next three days, we tarped more than fifty houses. For the next few weeks, I spent all day in the field making sales. It took time to get sales ramped up and jobs on the books, but by May 1, our office manager was working part-time from her home. By May 15, she was back in the office full-time helping me coordinate schedules and supplies.

Sometime in the middle of May, our sales guy was back on the job. He focused on sales for exterior work, and I shifted my focus to interior projects. On June 1, our designer returned. Of course, there were protocols to follow for both the interior and exterior jobs, but we didn't mind—we were back in business. By the end of June, things were running at what would become our new normal.

Crisis Is Coming

A crisis is coming. You can bet on it. Just like a tornado ripping through a community, you may not get much advance notice. One day you'll be rolling along, and then—*BAM!*—you get hit with something you never expected.

It may be something that affects your specific industry. For us, that was the housing market crash of 2008.

It might be something specific to your company, like the loss of key people who decide to move on to another organization.

It might be something personal, like an illness or a family emergency.

Or it might be something global, like a pandemic that shuts down the world and then disrupts the supply chain and creates shortages that lead to abrupt inflation.

Yeah, you can bet a crisis is coming, and how well you weather that storm depends largely on your ability to pivot.

Principle 9: Pivot

Entrepreneurs must be ready for anything, even unpredictable catastrophes. It sounds like an impossible task, but the truth is that sometimes a quick pivot can make the difference between bank-rolling or bankruptcy. Three key traits have helped our company pivot when necessary: being flexible, being proactive, and being debt-free.

Be Flexible

Prior to 2008, banks gave homeowners equity loans seemingly without question. Many of our customers used those loans to pay for new roofs or siding or for their kitchen or bath remodels. Some customers opted to take out a single, large loan and contract us for multiple projects at once.

Everything changed when the housing market crashed in October 2008. Suddenly, potential clients didn't have access to home equity loans for large projects. No longer could they afford to do a full kitchen remodel, much less a bath remodel, siding, windows, and a roof all at the same time.

With customers now having to pay for work out of pocket, we had to pivot. When I was on a sales call, I would still offer home-owners all the options, but I also acted as a consultant. By providing a menu of pricing for all the projects customers needed and then working with them to prioritize their needs, we retained customers for two to three years as, little by little, we worked our way down their needs list.

Had we been inflexible and stuck to the old way of doing things, our company would have suffered huge losses during that time. Instead, we were able to build long-lasting relationships with clients.

We practiced that flexibility again in 2021 when supply chain issues started to affect some of our long-time cabinetry vendors. Orders that used to take eight to ten weeks were now taking up to twenty-six weeks. We loved the products we'd been using, but we needed options for our clients who couldn't wait six months for their kitchen remodel to be completed.

Our design team evaluated other vendors' products, and we found a company that could deliver in ten weeks. We maintain the relationship we had with our existing vendor and order from them when we can, but having multiple choices has made it possible to stay on schedule with our clients.

Be Proactive

Aside from the stay-at-home order we were given in mid-March, the first quarter of 2020 had clicked along at a typical pace. Like everyone, we saw some price increases, but nothing to be concerned about. The second quarter was a different story. We were back to work at full speed, and inflation had escalated noticeably. Then the weakest links in the supply chain broke, and suddenly there were delays on all sorts of products (something that continues even as I'm writing this book).

It was time to pivot again. It was easy to see that the distribution issues weren't going to get resolved quickly, so this time, rather than waiting until we needed products, we decided to be proactive. For example, when we ordered pressure-treated lumber for jobs we anticipated doing in the months ahead, we bought much earlier than we normally would have, ordered in bulk, and paid cash. By doing so, we were able to avoid paying a significantly higher price, and we simply stored the extra lumber in our warehouse.

Anticipating upcoming needs is part of being proactive. We are (or I should say, Deanna is) strategic about saving for big purchases, like marketing expenses, vehicles for the business, equipment, or technology, and for maintenance and upkeep. Knowing the plan for the business and preparing for future needs keeps us from having to borrow funds.

We also put a percentage of every sale into what we call a slippage account. The funds in this account are there to cover mistakes. For example, if someone measures a window or cabinet incorrectly, we never ask the customer to pay for the replacement. If it's our mistake, then we cover it using the funds in our slippage account. These funds also allow us to reinvest in the company so we can stay ahead of the competition.

Be Debt-Free

Being debt-free and having cash available for supplies has saved us and our clients a significant amount of money. It has given us buying power that we simply wouldn't have had otherwise.

We have come so far from the days when I was robbing Peter to pay Paul. With Deanna as our CFO, except for the purchase of our building, we have remained debt-free. Because of her focus and intentionality, she knows exactly where we are financially at any given time. (Note: This illustrates why you've *got* to get the right people in place if you're going to be able to pivot.)

When we had to lay people off in 2020, knowing our numbers—what was in savings, what was outstanding, and what was coming in—gave us a complete picture of our financial standing. We had money set aside in savings that could cover expenses, at least for a while, and we could have used some of those funds to try to keep all, or at least some, people on staff. The problem was that we had no idea how long the stay-at-home order would last, and payroll was our biggest expense. Without any money coming in, it wouldn't be long before the savings were depleted, so we made the decision to temporarily close the business until we had enough work to start paying our employees again.

Being debt-free gave us the flexibility to pivot and allowed us to thrive. It also enabled us to stay afloat until we could get back to work. Even though we cut out our payroll expenses, there were still vendors to be paid for the jobs we were in the middle of, payments to make on our building, insurance, and other bills to be paid.

Times of crisis are packed with uncertainty and emotion, but being prepared to pivot makes it easier to weather the storms.

Application

- What would happen to your business if you were hit by a crisis?
- Do you have the insurance and savings in place to cover major losses or see your company through lean times?
- What could you do to be more proactive about potential pivots?

CONCLUSION
YOUR BUSINESS *AND* YOUR LIFE

I accepted Jesus as my Savior just a few years before I started Medina Exteriors. Prior to that time, I'd known about Jesus. I had grown up going to mass with my family, so God wasn't new to me. Feeling his call on my life, however, was wholly different. All at once, I recognized that I had been trying, futilely, to fill an emptiness in myself—in my soul. Jesus filled that void and began chipping away at my stubborn, prideful heart. I've been transparent about my growing pains in this book, so you know that process is ongoing.

I'm still a work in progress, but I knew from the very beginning that I wanted to honor God by running my company the right way. I wanted to do things ethically and to work with excellence. Integrity, character, and a mindset of abundance rather than scarcity are important to me, and so is treating people well.

From that first day in business until now, I have worked to make sure that our prices are fair and our estimates are accurate. I pay attention to the details of the job—labor costs, the quality of materials, projected time, and the overall budget—because I never take for granted that the customer is trusting me not only with their money but also with their homes. I knew that if I was going to make a real difference in my customers' lives, then I had to start by being honest, up front, and diligent. Since Day One, we have lived out our passion and focused on improving lives by improving homes.

In the same way, I know that the people who work for me deserve my very best. They deserve to be treated with respect. My aim has been to create a workplace where each person on the team can grow in their area of strength or unique ability. Many of our team members have been with us for years, which is unusual given the typically high turnover rate in the construction industry. Our team members stay because of the culture we've built. They stay because they feel like part of a team. Our company means more to them than a paycheck.

There's no getting around the fact that without profits businesses can't thrive, but money is a byproduct of what I do. I serve. I help people. I collaborate with others. That's what drives me.

Serving, helping, and collaborating are also my reasons for writing this book, creating a mastermind group, and developing the software we've been working so hard on. I do all those things because my end goal is to serve my industry and to serve my team members in a way that ignites their souls to become their best. When that happens, we all win.

The life of an entrepreneur is thrilling and terrifying, exciting and exhausting. It is worth every drop of sweat, blood, and tears you put into it. (And believe me, if you're working in the construction industry or any service-based, blue-collar trade, there will be plenty of all three.)

I don't know where you are on your journey, but my hope is that these nine principles will help smooth your learning curve so that it looks a little less like Mt. Everest. Being an entrepreneur is hard, and the climb to the top is often steeper than you imagined it would be, but if you apply the principles we've looked at in this book, then you'll be equipped with the right map, the right tools, and if you're interested, a plan to chart your way forward from a guide who knows the way.

9 Principles for Building a Business That Works for You

1. **Understand the Entrepreneurial Mindset**—If you're an entrepreneur, then chances are the traditional route doesn't feel right to you. Most people won't get you, but those who do will become some of your closest friends. (See Principle 5)

2. **Fail Frequently, Fail Fast, Fail Forward**—Marcus Aurelius said, "The impediment to action advances action. What stands in the way becomes the way."[8] In other words, challenges, and yes, even failures, are the way to success. Failure shows us what works and what doesn't. It pushes us onward and upward in our climb. Don't avoid trying something new just because there's a chance it won't work. Remember: If you fail to fail, then you've failed.

3. **Imperfect Action Pays Off**—You don't have to know the final step before you take the first one. It's okay if you don't know what step three looks like, and it's okay if step one is shaky. As President Truman said, "Imperfect action beats perfect inaction every time."

4. **Be a Student**—The humble learner will go further in life than any know-it-all. Find people who are a few steps ahead of you in the journey and ask questions. The knowledge and inspiration you gain from mentors, masterminds, and networking groups will accelerate your growth.

5. **Network and Apply What You Learn**—Find the people who get you. When like-minded, positive-thinking entrepreneurs gather, everyone brings something to the table. Join a group in your industry, or find a group with varied interests and the common goal of growth. Participate, listen, share, learn, and then adapt and apply the knowledge to your business.

6. **Do Whatever It Takes to Succeed**—When you've found your passion, pursue it with everything you've got. Don't quit or get derailed when challenges arise. Persevere!

Commit to doing whatever it takes to thrive, even if that means changing your approach or your mindset.

7. **Be Willing to Make Changes**—The way you start isn't the way you finish. As you learn from other entrepreneurs, implement what you glean, and share your experience. Decide what you want your company to look like and then do the work to make it a reality. It may require releasing those who don't fit your culture, but your company will be stronger for it.

8. **Learn, Collaborate, and Grow**—Develop a clear path for your team members to follow. Don't assume they already know. Equipping your people for success means giving them clear guidelines, setting expectations, and providing them with the training, processes, and technology they need.

9. **Pivot**—No business is immune to challenges. Be prepared to pivot by being flexible, proactive, and debt free. Planning ahead can save you money and frustration down the line— and just may save your business.

You are an entrepreneur, which means it's only natural that your path looks different from mine or anyone else's. My hope and prayer for you is that there will be enough challenges to push you to grow, enough mountain-top experiences to inspire you to keep climbing, and that you enjoy the life of abundance and time freedom that is waiting for you.

ABOUT THE AUTHOR

Brett Ruiz was born with an entrepreneurial spirit. From a young age, he knew that the status quo and the traditional career path weren't a fit for him. After a series of false starts and failures, Brett founded what is now Medina Exteriors & Remodeling + Simply Distinct Kitchens and Baths. During the past thirty years, Brett's company has weathered a number of storms—some of his own making and some, like the housing market crash and the pandemic, which were out of his control—but each time, they have come out stronger on the other side. Through perseverance and a commitment to innovation, he has learned how to build a thriving, self-managed business. Today, he uses that experience to mentor entrepreneurs as they launch and grow their own businesses.

Brett lives in Ohio with his wife, Deanna (who is also the CFO of his company), and their four children. When he's isn't in the office or on a sales call, Brett enjoys making the most of his time with his family.

RESOURCES

Below is a list of resources I've mentioned in this book as well as a few others that have been important to my growth as an entrepreneur.

Proof Management Networking Group—proofman.com
Strategic Coach©—strategiccoach.com
EOS Worldwide®—eosworldwide.com

Recommended Reading

AI as Your Teammate by Evan Ryan
Bold by Peter H. Diamandis and Steven Kotler
The E-Myth Revisited by Michael Gerber
Epic Business by Justin Breen
The Gap and The Gain by Dan Sullivan and Dr. Benjamin Hardy
Smart, Not Spoiled by Chad Willardson
Traction by Geno Wickman
Who, Not How by Dan Sullivan and Dr. Benjamin Hardy

BIBLIOGRAPHY

1 Juang, Mike. "A secret many small-business owners share with Mark Zuckerberg." CNBC.com. July 19, 2017. https://www.cnbc.com/2017/07/19/survey-shows-majority-of-business-owners-lack-college-degree.html.

2 Diamandis, Peter. "Google's 8 Innovation Principles." PeterDiamandis.com. November 3, 2014. https://www.diamandis.com/blog/googles-8-innovation-principles

3 Leong, Kathy Chin. "Google Reveals Its 9 Principles of Innovation." FastCompany.com. November 30, 2013. https://www.fastcompany.com/3021956/googles-nine-principles-of-innovation.

4 Godin, Seth. The Dip: A Little Book That Teaches You When to Quit (and When to Stick). New York: Penguin Group, 2007.

5 McIntyre, Georgia. "What Percentage of Small Businesses Fail? (And Other Need-to-Know Stats)." Fundera.com. November 20, 2020. https://www.fundera.com/blog/what-percentage-of-small-businesses-fail?

6 "What Is Your Unique Ability?" The Multiplier Mindset Blog. https://resources.strategiccoach.com/the-multiplier-mindset-blog/what-is-unique-ability. Accessed March 22, 2022.

7 Steve Jobs 1995 Interview NeXT Computer. https://vimeo.com/31813340?utm_campaign=5370367&utm_source=affiliate&utm_channel=affiliate&cjevent=f180ada5ad0c11ec802000e90a1c0e11&clickid=f180ada5ad0c11ec802000e90a1c0e11. Accessed March 2022.

8 Aurelius, Marcus. Meditations. https://www.gutenberg.org/files/2680/2680-h/2680-h.htm.